What Has a Water Tank and Wails?

UNCOVER & DISCOVER

WRITTEN BY **Robert Kanner**
ILLUSTRATED BY **Russ Daff**

dingles&company New Jersey

FOR MOM, MY BOOK MUSE

© 2008 dingles & company

ALL RIGHTS RESERVED
No part of this book may be reproduced in any form without written permission from the publishers, except by a reviewer who may quote brief passages in a review to be printed in a newspaper or magazine.

First Printing

Published by dingles&company
P.O. Box 508
Sea Girt, New Jersey 08750

**LIBRARY OF CONGRESS
CATALOG CARD NUMBER**
2007904586

ISBN
978-1-59646-844-3

Printed in the United States
of America

The Uncover & Discover series is based on the original concept of Judy Mazzeo Zocchi.

ART DIRECTION & DESIGN
Rizco Design

EDITORIAL CONSULTANT
Andrea Curley

PROJECT MANAGER
Lisa Aldorasi

EDUCATIONAL CONSULTANT
Melissa Oster and Margaret Bergin

CREATIVE DIRECTOR
Barbie Lambert

PRE-PRESS
Pixel Graphics

WEBSITE
www.dingles.com

E-MAIL
info@dingles.com

UNCOVER & DISCOVER

The **Uncover & Discover** series encourages children to inquire, investigate, and use their imagination in an interactive and entertaining manner. This series helps to sharpen their powers of observation, improve reading and writing skills, and apply knowledge across the curriculum.

Uncover each one and see you can when you're

clue one by what vehicle discover done!

My front end has different types of **red and yellow lights** that warn people to get out of my way.

LOOK FOR THE RED AND YELLOW LIGHTS.

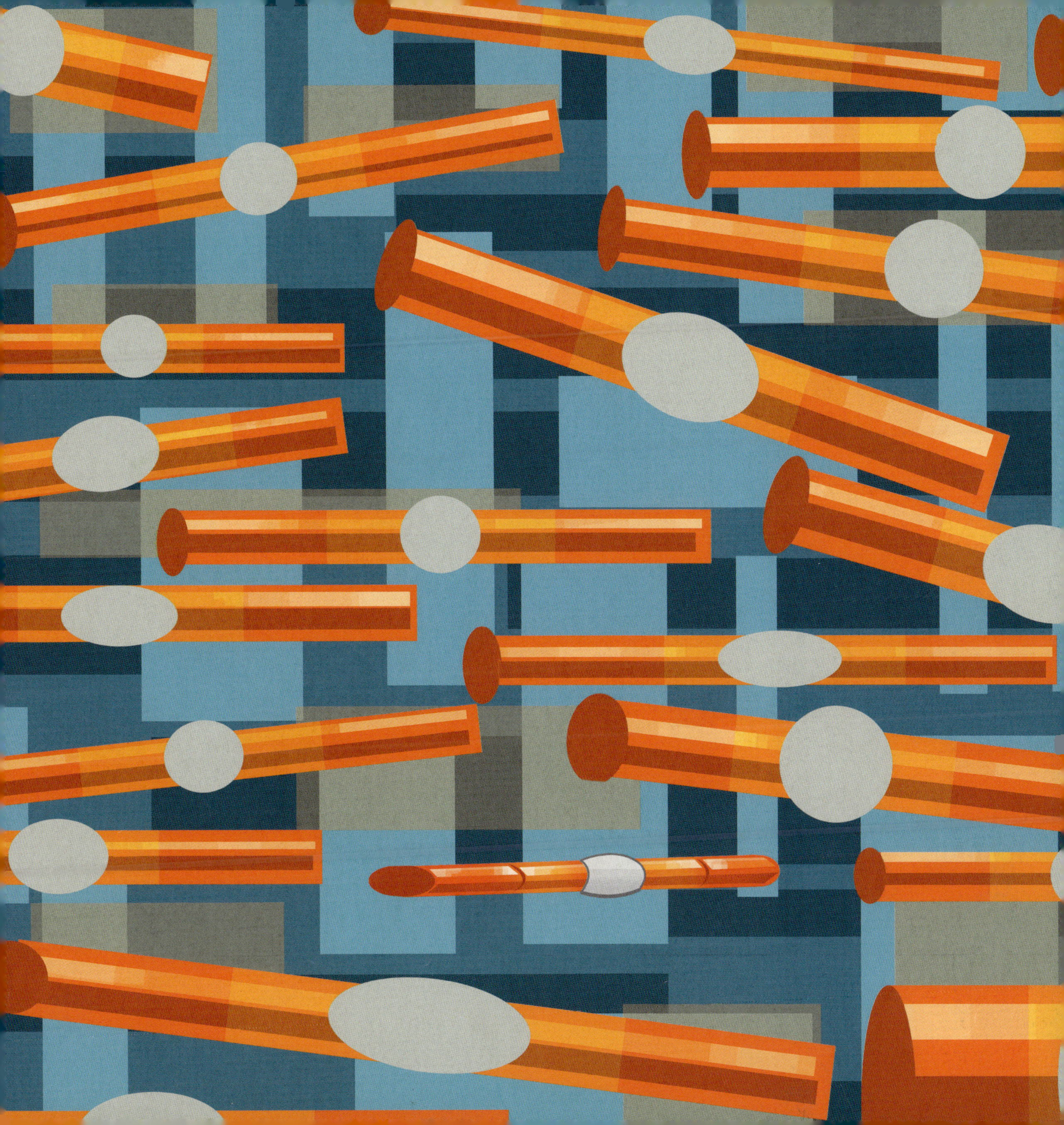

I carry **air packs** that my passengers can put on when they are in smoky places.

FIND THE **AIR PACK**.

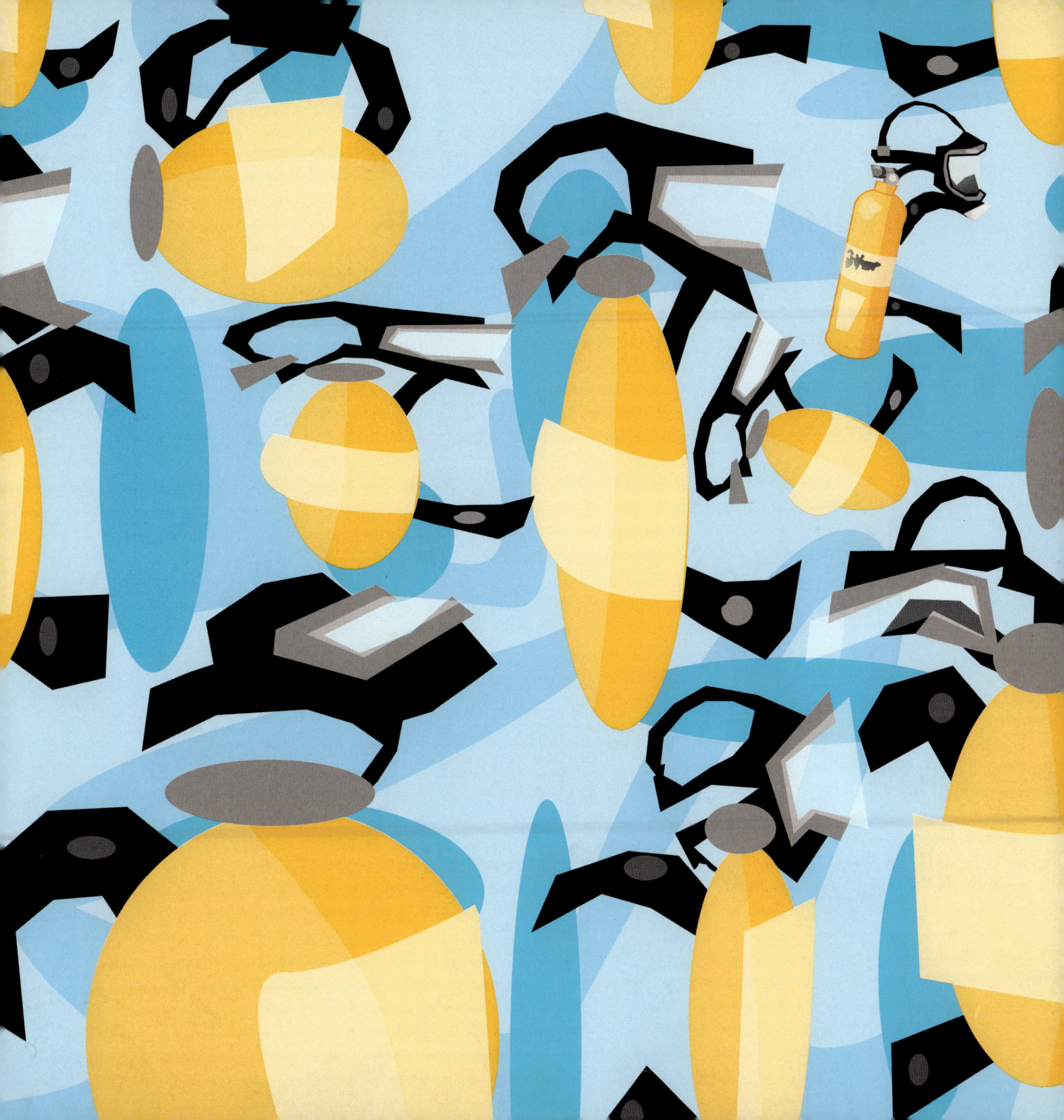

My first-aid equipment includes an emergency **oxygen tank** in case my passengers rescue people who need fresh air.

DO YOU SEE THE **OXYGEN TANK?**

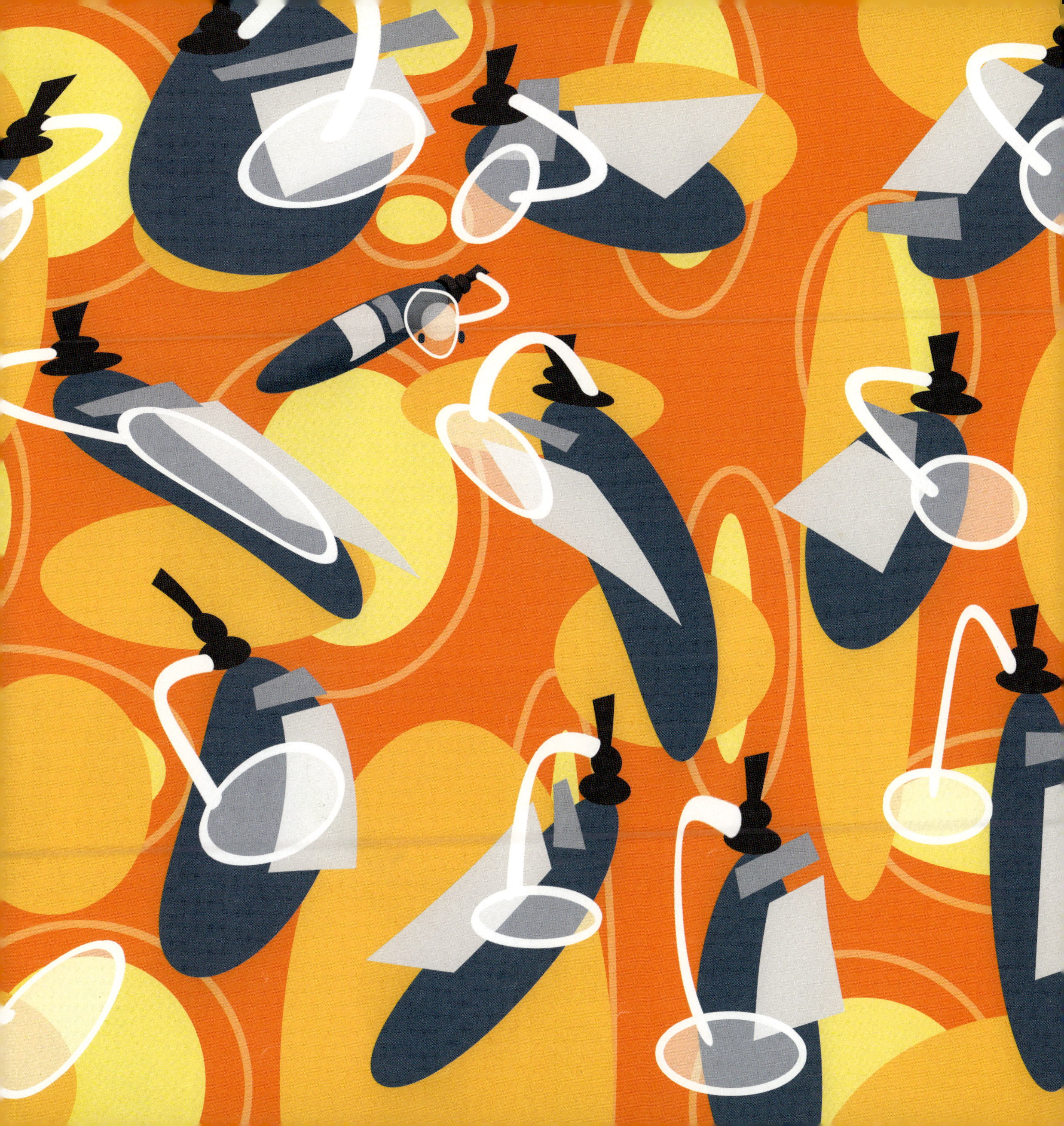

I also carry a **pike pole** that can be used to pull down a ceiling.

WHERE IS THE PIKE POLE?

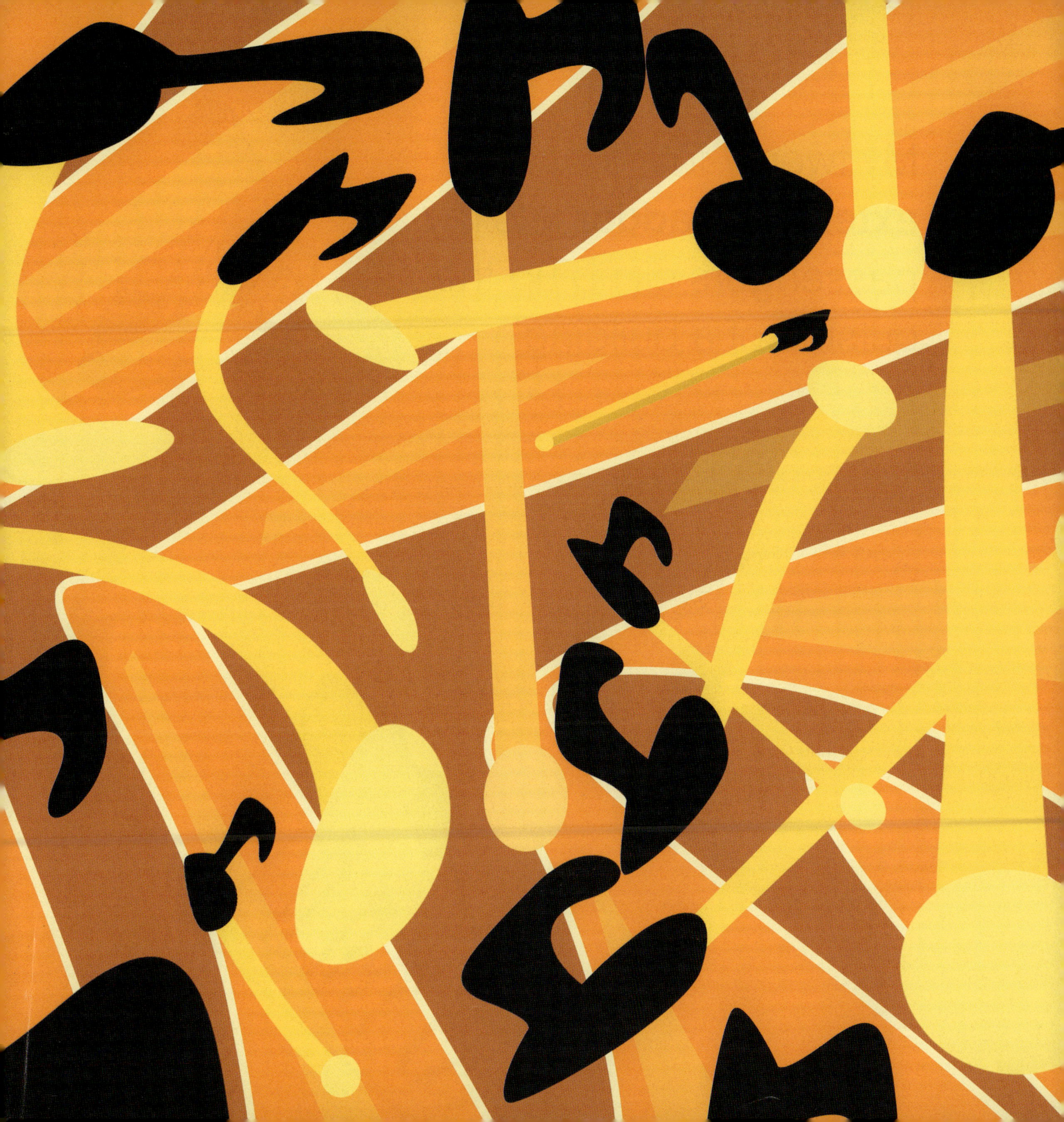

My twenty-four-foot **extension ladder** lets my passengers climb up the outside of a building.

LOOK FOR THE **EXTENSION LADDER**.

I have a **cab** where the driver, captain, and passengers sit.

WHERE IS THE **CAB**?

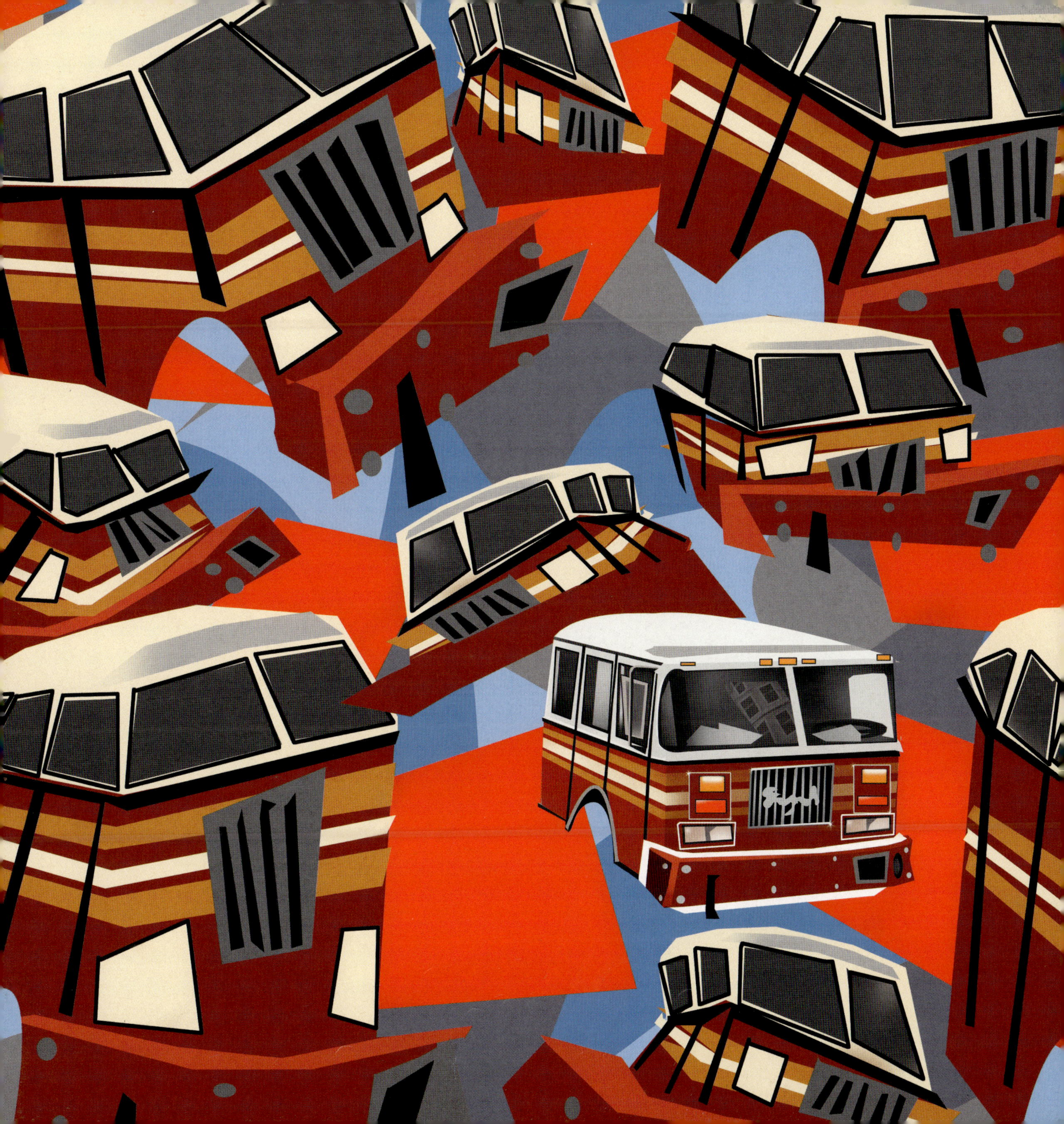

My passengers count on me to have an **exhaust fan** that can suck smoke and gases out of a building.

FIND THE **EXHAUST FAN**.

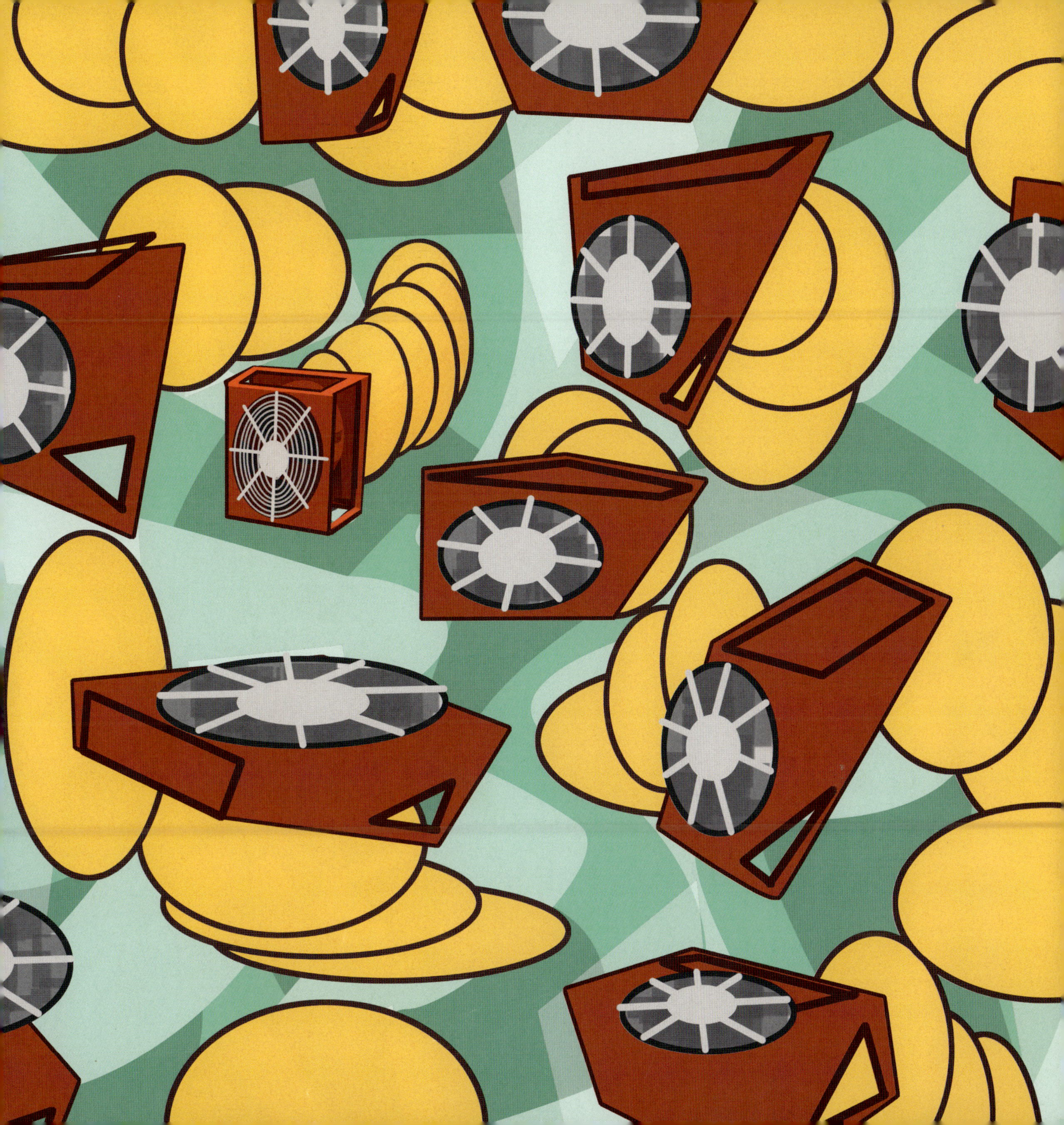

I carry several hundred feet of **hose** that can be hooked up to a fire hydrant.

DO YOU SEE THE **HOSE?**

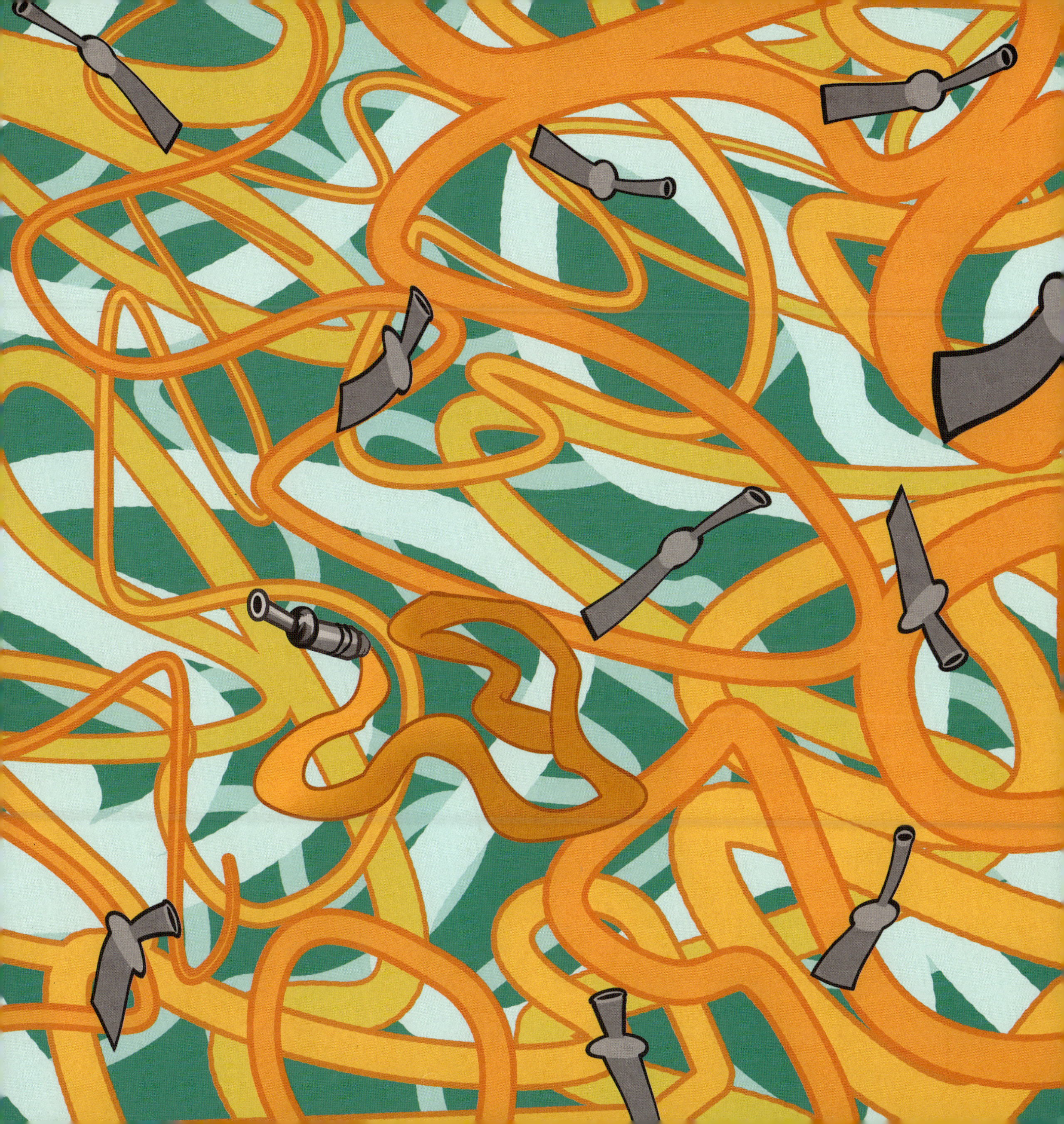

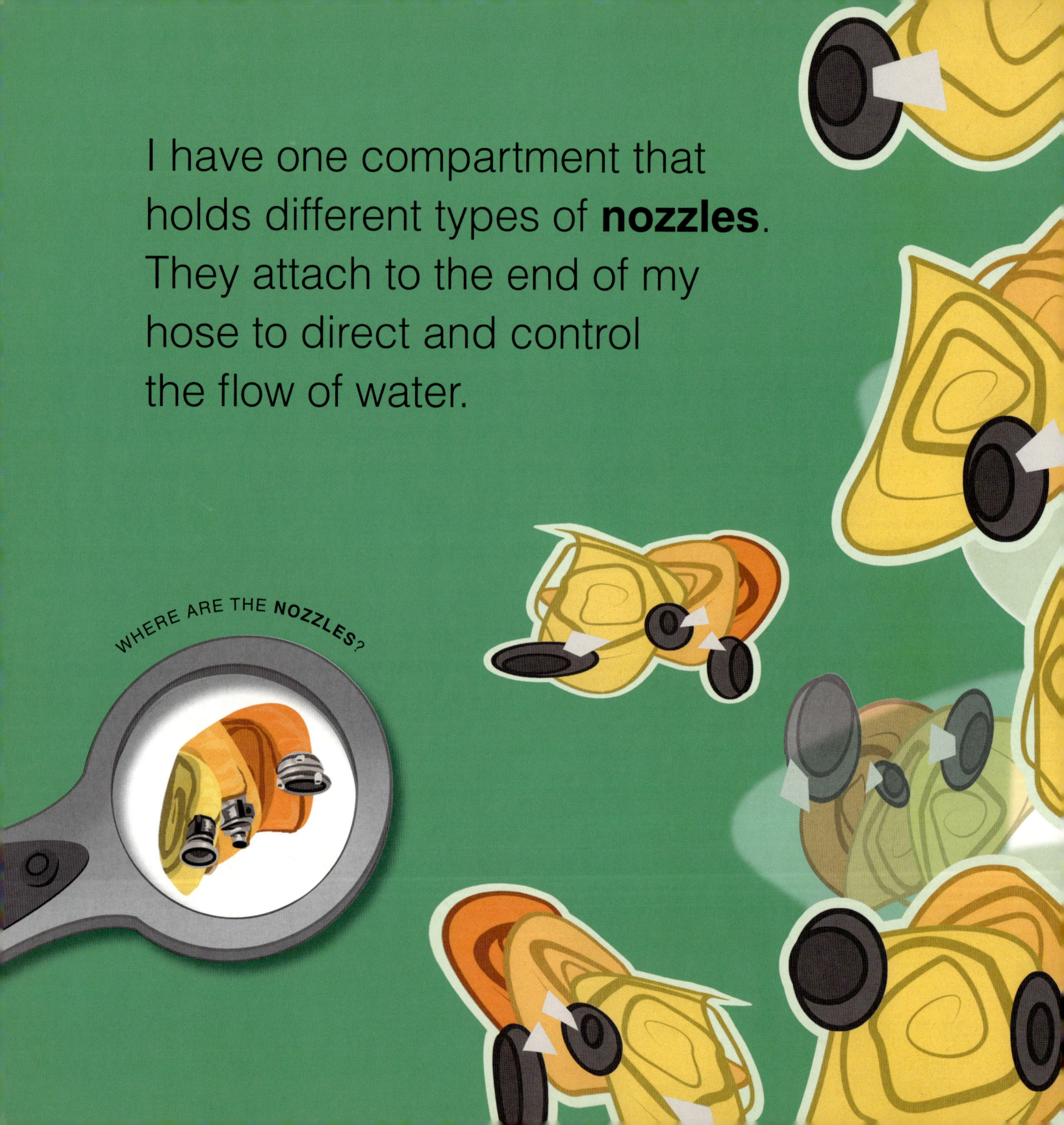

I have one compartment that holds different types of **nozzles**. They attach to the end of my hose to direct and control the flow of water.

WHERE ARE THE NOZZLES?

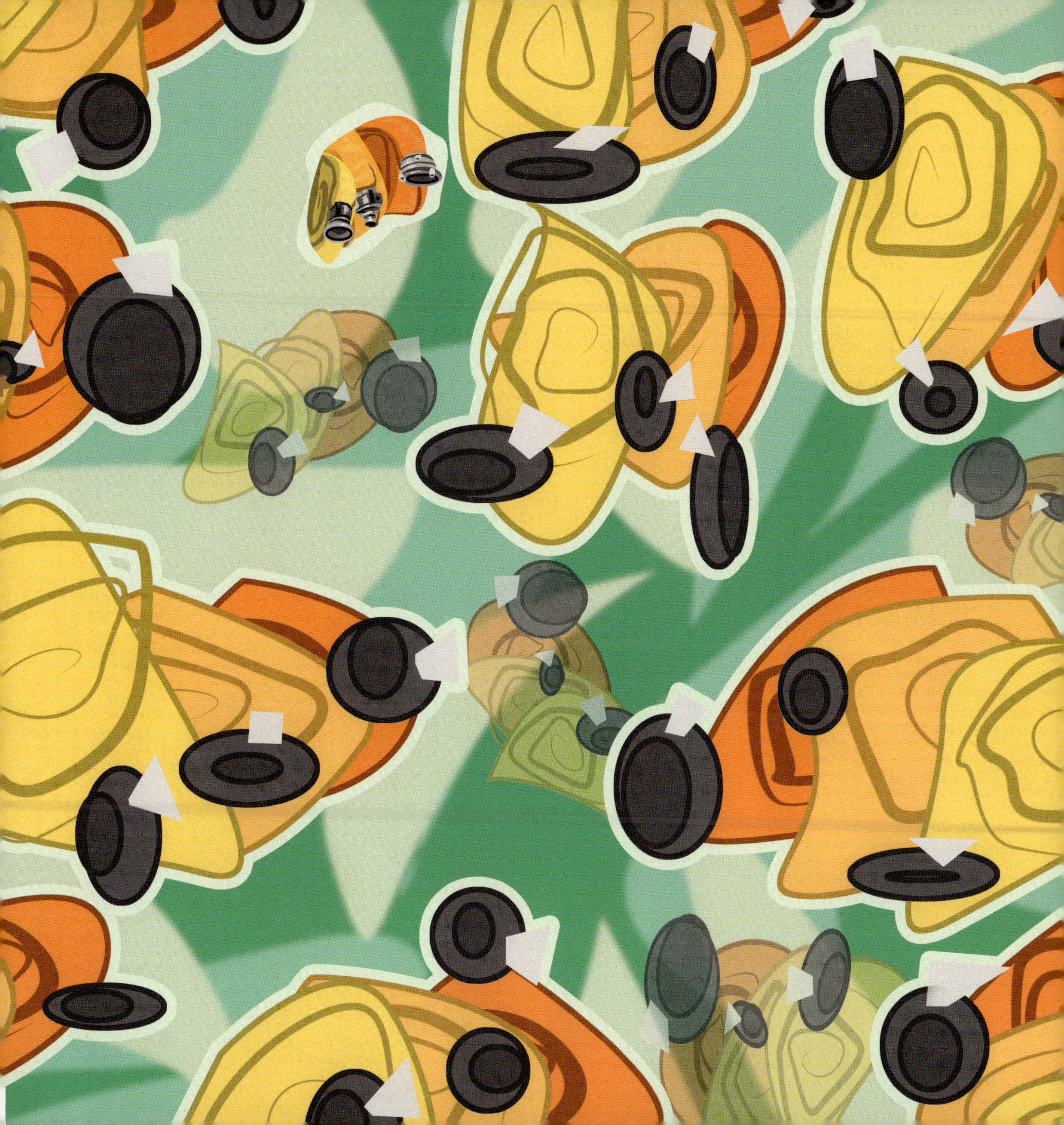

A **hydrant wrench** is always on board so my passengers can open a fire hydrant.

LOOK FOR THE **HYDRANT WRENCH**.

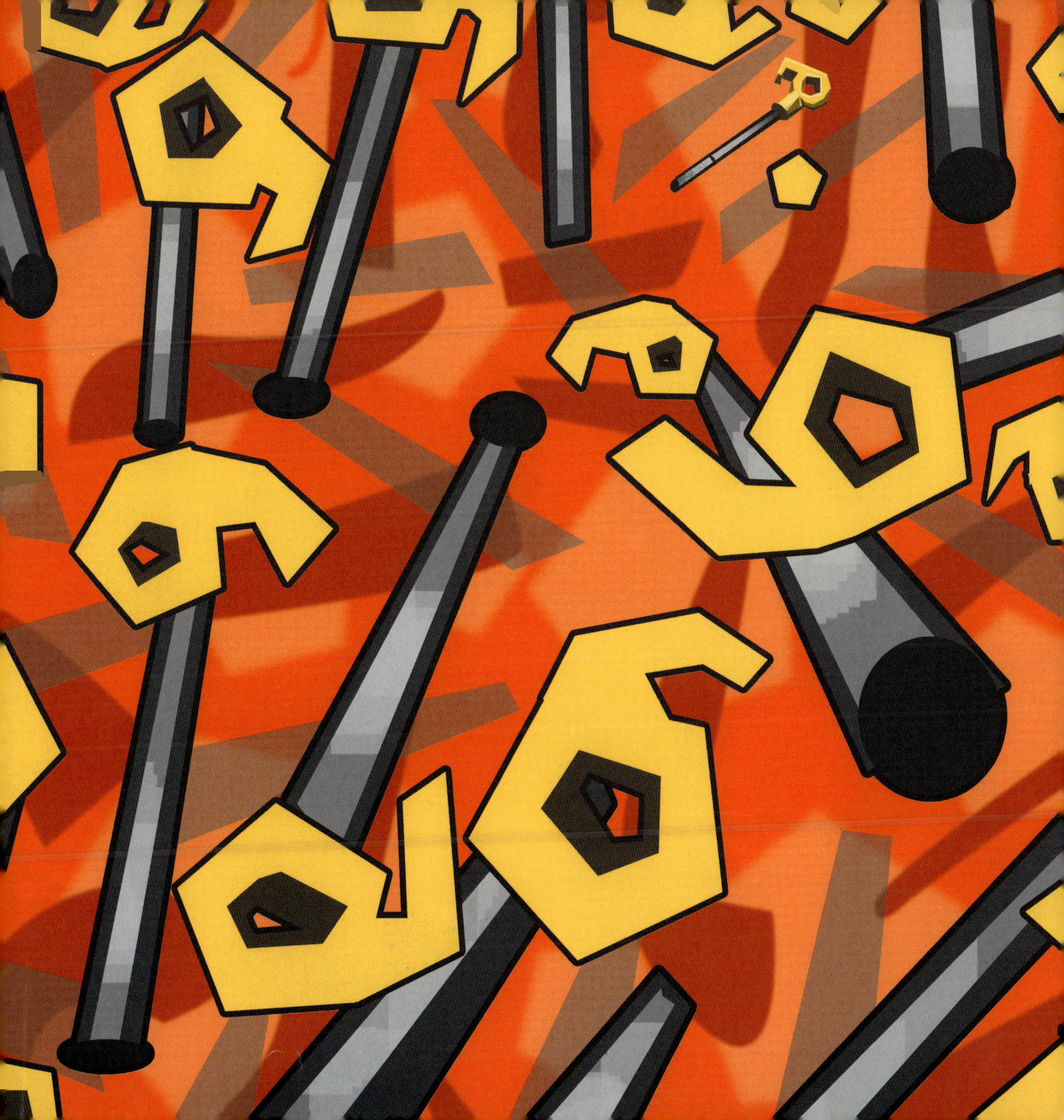

One of my compartments holds **salvage covers** that are used to keep water and smoke away from furniture.

FIND THE **SALVAGE COVER**.

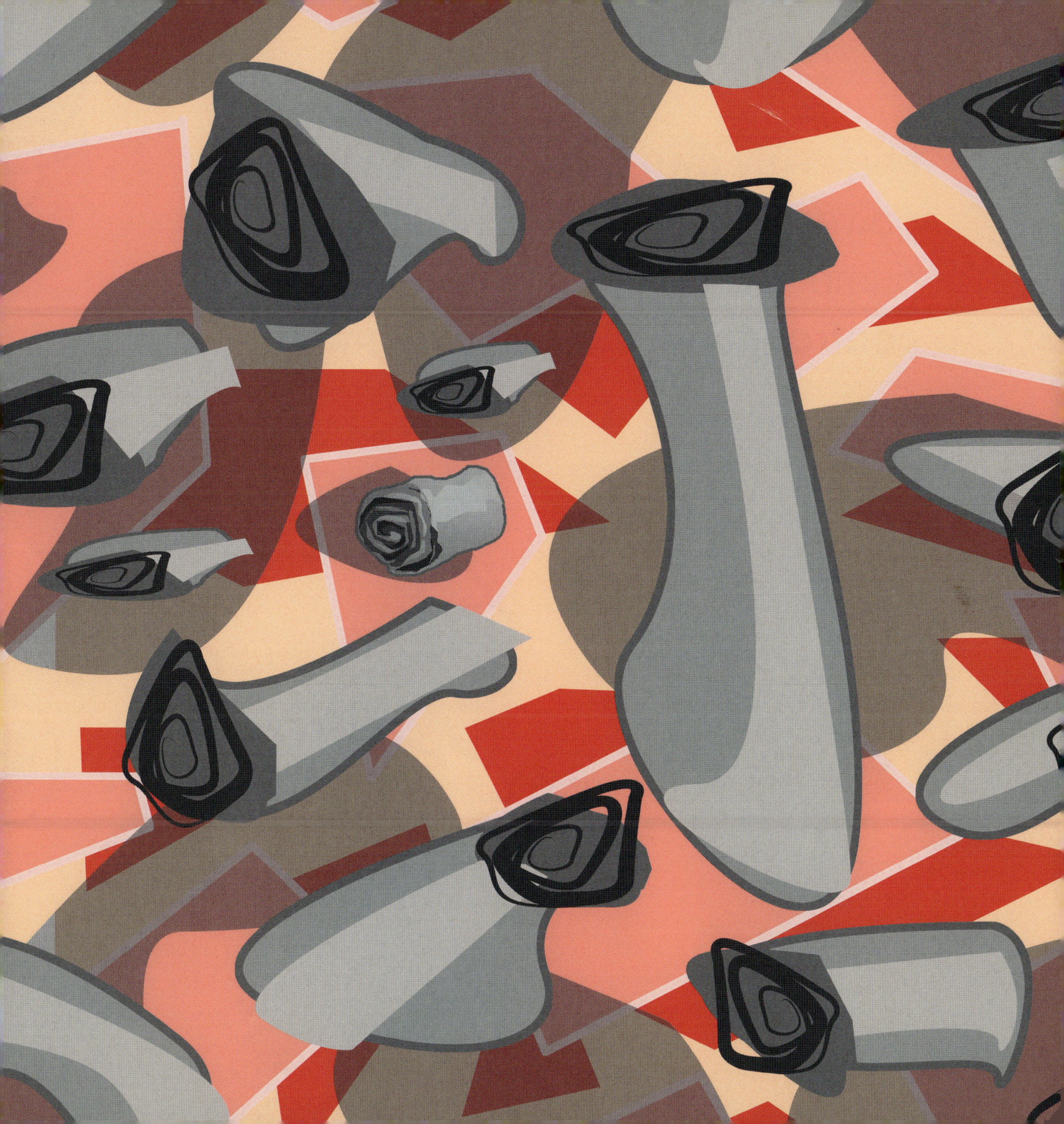

I have my own water tank and a powerful water pump. My water pump is operated from a **fire pump control panel** mounted on my side.

DO YOU SEE THE **FIRE PUMP CONTROL PANEL?**

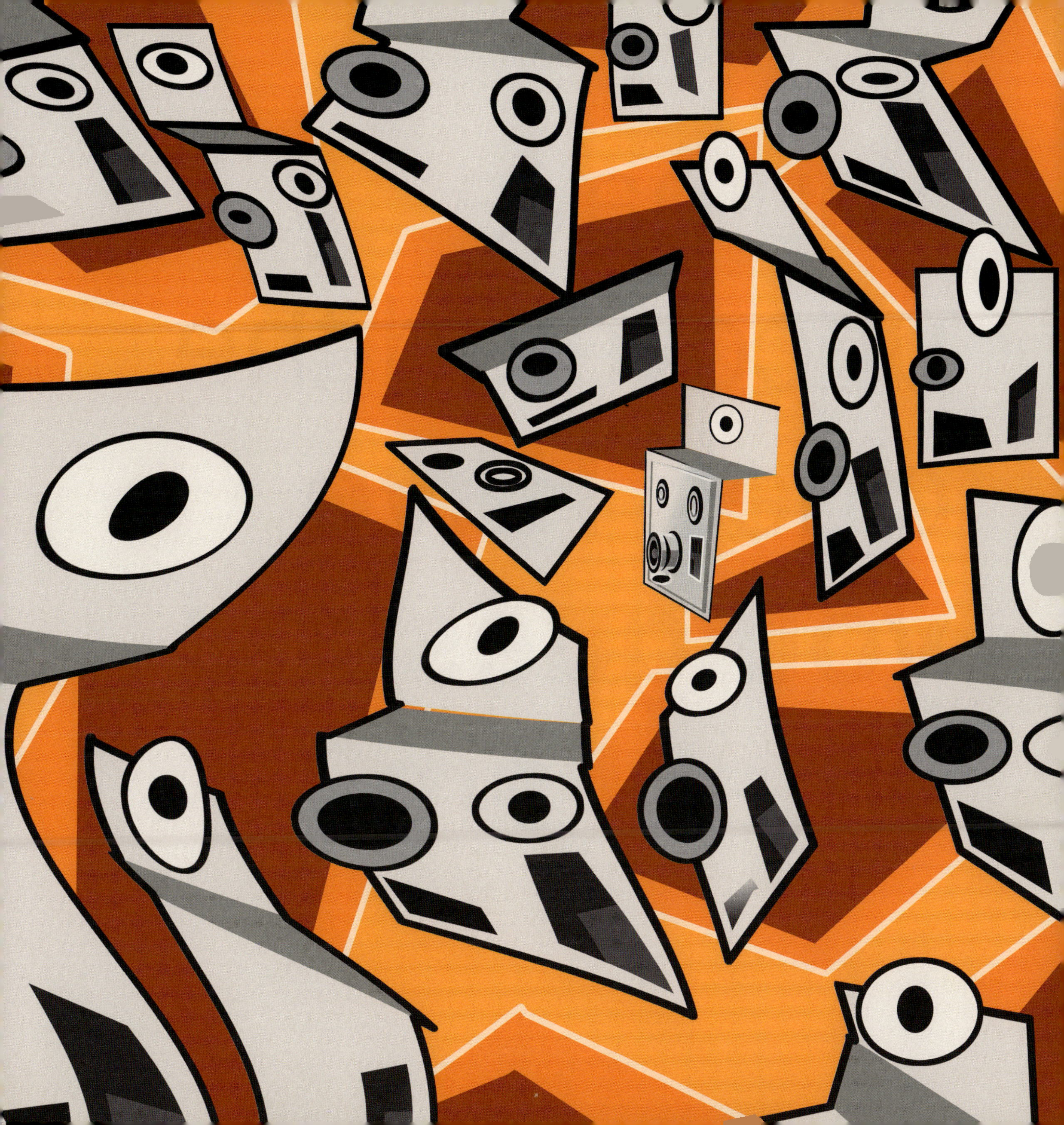

You have uncovered the clues. **Have you guessed what I am?**

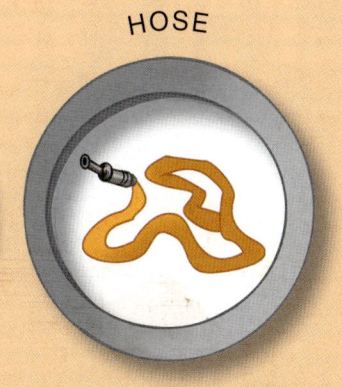

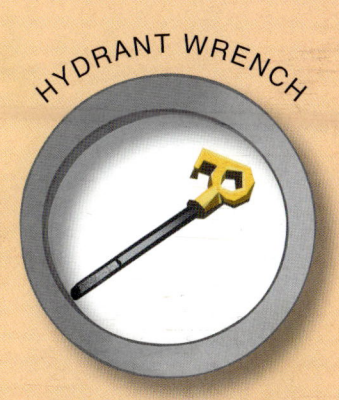

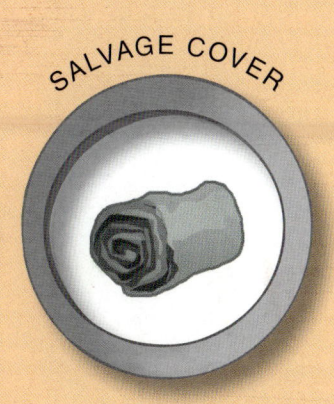

RED AND YELLOW LIGHTS	**AIR PACK**	**OXYGEN TANK**	**PIKE POLE**
EXTENSION LADDER	**CAB**	**EXHAUST FAN**	**HOSE**
NOZZLES	**HYDRANT WRENCH**	**SALVAGE COVER**	**FIRE PUMP CONTROL PANEL**

If not, here are more clues.

1. I am one of a group of vehicles called fire apparatus. Each of us is designed for a special task. I am a pumper. I have a water tank, a pump, and a place to store my hoses. I am used mainly to pump water.

2. My cab can seat up to 8 firefighters. A driver and a captain sit in my front seat. Up to 6 firefighters can sit in my jump seat area, which is like the backseat of a car.

3. I weigh about 35,000 pounds, about the same weight as a bus.

4. My water tank holds 1,000 gallons of water. That is about 20 bathtubs full of water.

5. My pump can pump out 1,000 gallons of water a minute. About 6 gallons of water come out of a showerhead in the same amount of time!

6. When I arrive at a fire, my firefighters locate a fire hydrant. They attach my hoses to it so that I have a nonstop supply of water. If a hydrant isn't available, I use my onboard water supply.

7. In order to get to a fire quickly, I flash my red and yellow lights and turn on my loud, blaring siren. When I do this, I am allowed to go through red lights, travel on the wrong side of the road, and go very fast.

8. My parts are made of steel, aluminum, and rubber.

Now add them up and you'll see...

I'm a **Fire Engine** and you discovered me!

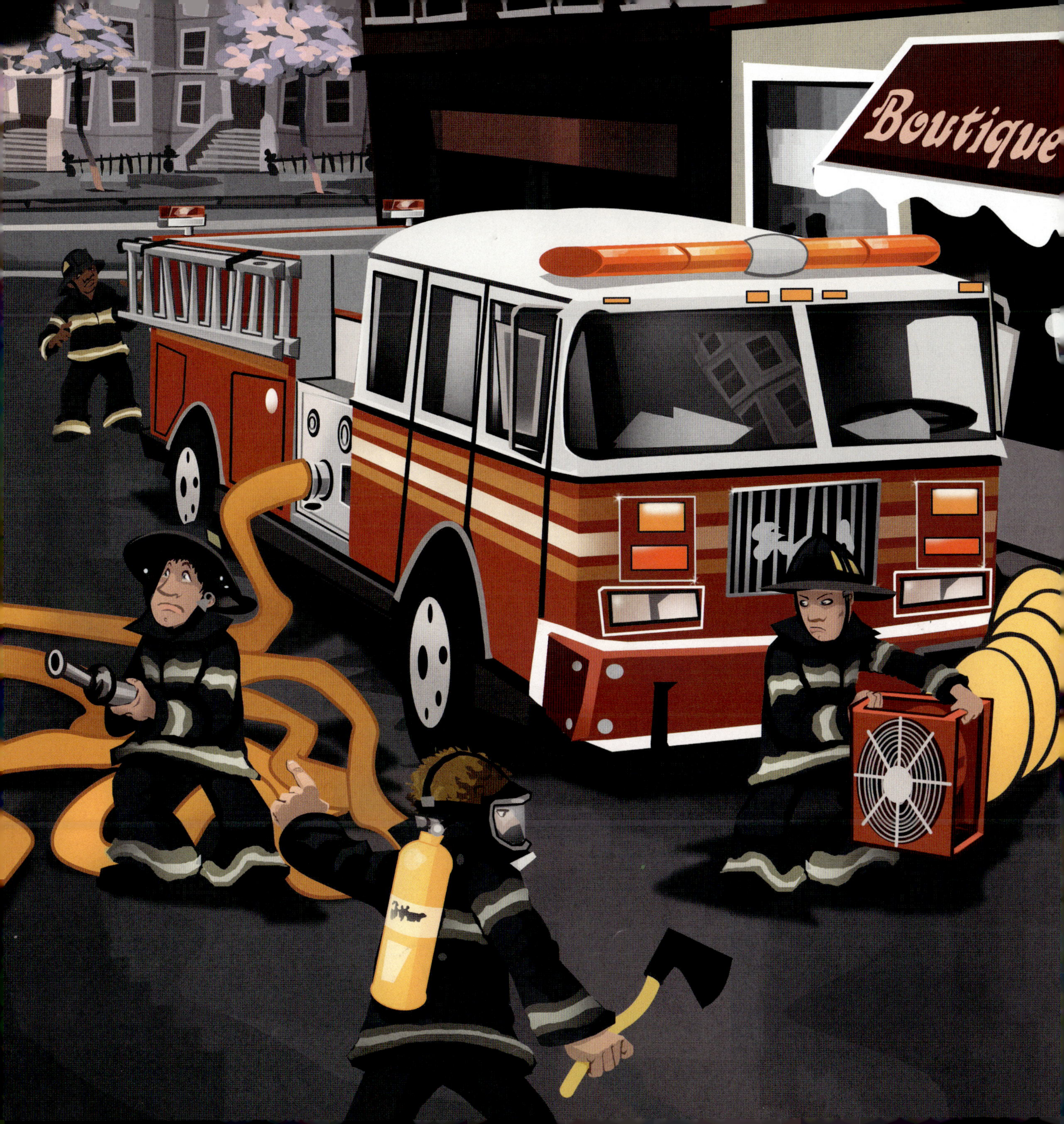
Boutique

Do you want to know more about me? Here are some Fire Engine fun facts.

1. The first fire apparatus used in the United States was the hand pumper. It was built in England and shipped by boat to New York during the early 1700s.

2. Steam pumpers were invented in the 1800s. The pumper was pulled to the fire by 6 or 8 firefighters using a long rope.

3. In 1906 the Radnor Fire Company of Wayne, Pennsylvania, made a vehicle with two gasoline engines. One engine moved the vehicle and one powered the pump. This motorized pumper greatly improved the way fires were fought.

4. At first a bell on the fire engine alerted people to get out of the way. In 1913 a hand-cranked siren was introduced.

5. The Hall of Flame Museum in Phoenix, Arizona, has one of the earliest fire engines—from 1725. A crew of 20 worked its handles and foot pedals to pump about 60 gallons per minute through its copper nozzle.

Who, What, Where, When, Why, and How

USE THE QUESTIONS who, what, where, when, why, and how to help the child apply knowledge and process the information in the book. Encourage him or her to investigate, inquire, and imagine.

In the Book...

DO YOU KNOW WHO operates a fire engine?

DO YOU KNOW WHAT the featured vehicle in the book is?

DO YOU KNOW WHERE a fire engine is kept when it's not in use?

DO YOU KNOW WHEN a fire engine is needed?

DO YOU KNOW WHY a fire engine has a water tank?

DO YOU KNOW HOW a fire engine warns people to get out of its way?

In Your Life...

Have you ever been inside a firehouse? Ask a parent if you can visit your local firehouse.

CROSS-CURRICULAR EXTENSIONS

Math

There is a fire in the basement of a house and 3 fire engines respond. Because it is a small fire, 2 fire engines are not needed and they leave. A 4th fire engine shows up to check on the fire. How many fire engines are at the scene now?

Science

Some fires, such as electrical and chemical fires, cannot be put out with water. Do some research to find out how firefighters put out these types fires and what they use.

Social Studies

Firefighters have many responsibilities and duties. Do some research and learn what they include.

Fun Activity

You have uncovered the clues and discovered the fire engine. Now imagine you are a firefighter on duty.

ASSIGNMENT
Write a story about you and your fellow firefighters as you respond to a fire.

INCLUDE IN YOUR STORY
Who is driving the fire engine?
What type of gear are you wearing?
Where is the fire?
When will you arrive at the fire?
Why did the fire start?
How many fire engines are on the scene?

WRITE
Enjoy the writing process while you take what you have imagined and write your story.

UNCOVER & DISCOVER

Author

Robert Kanner is part of the writing team for the Uncover & Discover series as well as the Global Adventures and Holiday Happenings series. An extensive career in the film and television business includes work as a film acquisition executive at the Walt Disney Company, a story editor for a children's television series, and an independent family-film producer. He holds a bachelor's degree in psychology from the University of Buffalo and lives in the Hollywood Hills, California, with Tom and Miss Murphy May.

Illustrator

Since graduating from Falmouth School of Art in 1993, **Russ Daff** has enjoyed a varied career. For eight years he worked on numerous projects in the computer games industry, producing titles for Sony PlayStation and PC formats. While designing a wide range of characters and environments for these games, he developed a strong sense of visual impact that he later utilized in his illustration and comic work. Russ now concentrates on his illustration and cartooning full-time. When he is not working, he enjoys painting, writing cartoon stories, and playing bass guitar. He lives in Cambridge, England.